THE ESTHER EFFECT

THE ESTHER EFFECT

How to Recognize the Queen in You

Ariona Alexis Anderson

Printing Partners, Inc.

Author: Ariona Alexis Anderson
Foreword: Hope Bowers
Afterword: Alecia M. White

Unless otherwise noted, Scripture quotations are taken from the *Holy Bible*, New Living Translation, copyright © 1996, 2004, 2015 by Tyndale House Foundation. Used by permission of Tyndale House Publishers, Inc., Carol Stream, Illinois 60188. All rights reserved.

Scripture quotations marked *NLT* are from the *Holy Bible*, New Living Translation, copyright © 1996, 2004, 2015 by Tyndale House Foundation. Used by permission of Tyndale House Publishers, Inc., Carol Stream, Illinois 60188. All rights reserved.

Printed in the United States of America
Cover Design by: JayAmi Sellers

Printing Partners
929 W 16th Street
Indianapolis, IN 46202
PrintingPartners.net

ISBN: 978-1-949702-00-2
Copyright Number 1-6882398411

The Esther Effect: How to Recognize the Queen in You

For more information, please visit www.ArionaAAnderson.com

To every girl who was told that she was more pauper than Queen.
To every woman who is traveling on the road towards becoming her best self.
To the best mother and grandmother any young woman could ever ask for.
And to my Lord and Savior, Jesus Christ, to whom all glory belongs.

Contents

Foreword

I remember how I felt the day that I brought Ariona home from the hospital. I was so full of uncertainty about our future. I was a young mother that did not like children, and here I was with a baby. I knew that I had a responsibility to teach her to be the best "Ariona" that she could possibly be.

From an early age, Ariona had always been obsessed with the idea of being a Queen. This fixation started when she was about 5 years old when we watched Cleopatra starring Elizabeth Taylor. She was infatuated with Cleopatra so much so, that she began to mimic her behavior. For example, when Ariona would take a bath, she would draw the curtain back and yell "the Queen is bathing!" I would respond and call her Queen Ari and become her servant. It's something special to be able to serve your children. A servant is a devoted and helpful supporter. Some may think that this is a little much, but God has called us *all* to be servants to each other because He is the perfect example of a servant.

It wasn't until Ariona was about 9 years old that she discovered the story of Queen Esther. She immediately fell in love with the story and as she grew older, she would always say that Esther was her favorite.

Now imagine me, walking around with a child who was obsessed with this notion of being a Queen, while I, as a single mother, was still struggling to find the Queen within myself. I began to wonder, how could I encourage her to develop the Queen within herself, if I could not do it for my own self? I always tried to shower her with compliments and teach her that God said that she was beautifully and wonderfully made (Psalm 139:14). I wanted her to know that inside, she was meant to be a Queen and that she had inherited her crown by being God's baby.

After reading this book, I realized that I really am the mother of a Queen. She has been a blessing to me both naturally and spiritually. I have truly learned so much from her. While I was reading this book, I went to search for and dust off my own crown. And now, I feel more enlightened about my responsibility to encourage those I will encounter. I have found a renewed peace in being myself and I have put on my armor and I am ready to engage in battle.

I have learned that you will be able to accomplish much more in life when you realize that *you* are needed; not the broken you, but the undiscovered Queen within you.

I admonish you to go forth, find your crown, and wear it with grace and humility and get ready to engage the warrior within you.

- Hope Bowers -

Preface

The story of Esther has always been my absolute favorite story in the Bible. I am not sure if it was the favor over Esther's life, her courage to admit that she was afraid of God's call on her life, or her ability to obey God despite her fears, that made me fall in love with this story. However, as I have grown in my relationship with Christ, I now understand why the story of Esther held such an immense place in my heart; because, I now realize that, *I am Esther.*

I recognize now that there is an Esther that lives on the inside of every woman of faith. Through this faith filled journey, we will each come to a place where we will be captured by purpose, have our names changed, and be forced to make some of the most critical decisions of our lives all for the glory of God. I have found that many women come to a crossroads and have to determine whether they will wear their royal garments or be paralyzed by their own sense of unworthiness and the fear of what others might think.

My prayer is that you will see reflections of your own journey through this analysis of the story of Esther. And I pray that, through her story, you will find the strength and courage to walk into your God-given purpose.

I truly believe that there is something in this book that every woman can relate to and I thank you for taking the time to embark on this journey towards Queendom with me. I pray that God blesses you and allows your heart to be receptive and your spiritual eyes to be opened as you begin your journey towards becoming the Queen that the Father has always called you to be.

Queen, I salute you!

Introduction

So, what is the "Esther Effect"? Well I'm glad you asked! To me, the "Esther Effect" can be defined as the following: the result of the transformation a Christian woman undergoes after she recognizes who she is in Christ; the process by which a woman of faith elevates from living as Hadassah to walking in her Esther-like/Queenly authority; the revelation and activation of purpose in the daughters of Zion.

Now, I recognize that everyone who is reading this book may not be familiar with the story of Esther. Not to worry, I've got your back! The book of Esther is 10 chapters long and found in the Old Testament of the Bible. While the book is not particularly lengthy, it is filled with action, suspense, love, faith, and family. The primary "characters" at play in this book are: King Ahasuerus, the King (obviously, ha!); Vashti, the "ex-Queen"; Hadassah or Esther, the book's namesake and heroine; Mordecai, Esther's cousin and guardian, and; Haman, the Agagite and villain. In short, the book of Esther is the story of a young Jewish woman who, through unforeseen circumstances, became the Queen of Persia. And through a selfless and courageous act of faith, saved an entire nation of people from the threat of mass genocide that was orchestrated by one of the King's noblemen. Whew! Ok, now let's talk about the structure of the book.

At the beginning of each chapter you will find two things, the theme scripture(s) and the "Chapter

Breakdown" section. The theme scripture(s) will give you insight as to what the focus of any given chapter will be. Also, to give you context for the analysis in the proceeding text, the "Chapter Breakdown" sections will provide a brief synopsis of nearly everything that took place in that particular chapter in the book of Esther.

At the end of each chapter, there is a "Prayer" and a "Just in Case You Forgot" scriptural reference section. The "Prayer" section contains a brief prayer for you to repeat and meditate on. The "Just in Case You Forgot" section gives you positive affirmations and scripture references, for those times when you feel low and need to be reminded of who God says that you are. I am a very strong believer that life and death are in the power of the tongue (Proverbs 18:21). In other words, I believe that we can actually become the women that we say we are. Which is why the "Prayer" and "Just in Case You Forgot" sections are great ways for you to both petition the Father about how to become a better woman of faith and to prophesy to your own self about who God says that you are.

I am so excited and truly honored to be going on this journey with you. I hope and pray that this book blesses you and gives you the wisdom that you need to begin your journey towards recognizing the Queen inside of you.

Now, my Beautiful Sister, it is time for you to dust off your crown, put on your royal garments, and walk like the Queen that God ordained you to be!

What's in a Woman?

Esther 1:16-18 NLT. [16] Memucan answered the King and his nobles, "Queen Vashti has wronged not only the King but also every noble and citizen throughout your empire. [17] Women everywhere will begin to despise their husbands when they learn that Queen Vashti has refused to appear before the King. [18] Before this day is out, the wives of all the King's nobles throughout Persia and Media will hear what the Queen did and will start treating their husbands the same way. There will be no end to their contempt and anger.

Chapter 1 Breakdown

At the beginning of our story, we find King Ahasuerus throwing a large feast for all of the princes and servants in Susa. This seven-day shindig was going so well that the King decided that he wanted to show off his beautiful Queen, Vashti, to all of the people at the palace. But, when the King summoned her, she refused to come to the party. The King was furious, and he asked his fellow noblemen what he should do about the situation. The noblemen told the King that Vashti did not just sin against the King, but that Vashti had sinned against the entire kingdom. The noblemen were afraid that word would begin to spread throughout the kingdom about what Vashti had done. They were even more afraid that the women throughout the kingdom would follow in Vashti's footsteps and begin to dishonor their husbands. So, in order to stop utter chaos from ensuing amongst the people, the noblemen suggested that Vashti never be allowed to come before the King again, and that a new Queen be found to take her place.

So, what's in a woman? Well, I'll tell you! Strength, Authority, and Influence beyond measure. My Sister, it is imperative that you recognize the levels of power, authority and influence that lie within you before you begin your journey towards Queendom.

How do I know this? Just look at the text! The noblemen were afraid that the actions of this one woman would create complete and utter chaos throughout the entire kingdom. That's a lot of people! More importantly, that's a lot of *different* people. What do I mean by different?

The Bible says that King Ahasuerus ruled over 127 provinces and that these provinces ranged from India to Ethiopia. The King ruled over people from different ethnic, religious, cultural and economic backgrounds. And the social climate across the globe during Biblical times amongst different tribes, religious groups, and social classes was far more polarized and exclusive than they are today. Given those facts, you would think that the noblemen would not be worried about the level of influence one group would have over another. But, notice that the noblemen never said, "We should be afraid because the women in Susa will mimic Vashti's behavior. But the women in Ethiopia probably will not." Or, "The women who worship the same god(s) as Vashti will probably follow her lead. But the other women will disregard her actions." No! These noblemen were afraid that *all* of the women under the King's rule would be affected by what Vashti had done.

What does this mean? It means that the noblemen recognized that the influence that Vashti had superseded cultural, economic, religious and traditional norms. They understood that this one woman's actions had the potential to impact the entire kingdom! My Sister, the enemy fights you so hard with low self-esteem, discord amongst your fellow Sisters, and physical, mental and emotional oppression because he knows that if you were to ever truly realize your own God given strength, authority and influence, you would turn this world upside down! The authority to change nations, cultures, religious traditions, and governments is in your hands and rests over your life!

You are a dangerous force to be reckoned with and the enemy knows it and believe it or not, *he is terrified of you.* Your strength, your influence and your authority stretch far beyond any cultural, social, economic, ethnic or racial divide that society wants you to think separates you from your Sister. As a woman, by nature, you are granted a level of access and dominion that is different from that of any man's. Now, before I go further, I want to make this clear, this is not a book about women being better than men, nor is this a book whose aim is to put men down! If that is what you are looking for, I am not sorry to disappoint you. I am *not* saying that we are better than men, but, I am saying that there are some arenas that only we can operate in, some tasks that only we can perform and some anointings that only we bear. And get this, God specifically chose you to embark on this journey as a woman!

Please do not be mistaken, we serve a very intentional God. Which means that your gender was chosen on purpose. In Jeremiah 1:5, God says, "I knew you before I formed you in your mother's womb. Before you were born I set you apart and appointed you as my prophet to the nations." Like Jeremiah, even before you were born, God had already predestined you with a specific purpose. And once He assigned you with that purpose, He also decided that that purpose should be embodied by a woman and He made you! You were literally called and predestined by God to be a woman. How cool is that!

You must train yourself to stop thinking that you are strong or have power in spite of the fact that you are a woman and believe that you are strong and powerful *because* God ordained you to be a woman! The power does not lie in the gender, the power lies in the Savior! As a woman of God, the same signs that Mark 16:17 talks about that will follow those that believe, like healing the sick, raising the dead, casting out devils; along with the power to reach the throne of grace in prayer, to tread upon serpents and to move mountains all reside in you as a child of the Almighty God!

There is a major misconception within the body of Christ, and within society at large, that the only relevant positions that the women can operate in are "wife" and "mother". And while marriage and motherhood are beautiful callings that God has bestowed upon *some* women (because contrary to popular belief, I do believe that some women may not be called to be married or bear children), it is imperative that the average Christian woman (single or married, with or without children) recognizes that God has created her with a purpose in mind that includes serving Him and bringing honor and glory to His name before all others.

The goal of this book is to help you realize that there is ministry and value inside of you just as you are. There is a work to be done that God has specifically designed for your hands to do. Now, when I say ministry, please do not mistake me for saying that you are called to stand in the pulpit and preach. Now, that very well could be your calling, but your ministry could also lie in the way that you dance, paint, sing, write poems, do other people's hair or makeup, teach, care for your patients or clients, manage your staff, and so much more. Your ministry is deeply rooted in where your greatest passion lies.

Now, I know that stereotypes would categorize us women as being overly sensual or seductive and that we have, more often than not, been compared to the women in the Bible with negative storylines like Delilah and Jezebel. And yes, because we have the power of influence inside of us, we must be careful not to use it to cause our brothers and sisters to fall! However, it is not the Father's intention that rather than seeing yourself has His beloved daughter that you view yourself as being an evil, sinful temptress!

My Sister, *you* are the apple of God's eye! He has invested so much into you and now it is time for you to recognize your own value and understand who you truly are in Christ. You are not worthless, you are not a door mat, you are not dumb, and you carry significance long before you ever become someone's wife or mother. You are a favor bearer. You are a praiser and a worshipper. You are a *powerful* woman of substance filled with purpose and overflowing with grace! You have great *authority* and you possess the ability to do amazing things in the kingdom of God. And your *influence* stretches far beyond any social, religious or racial barriers this world tries to throw at you!

You are a force to be reckoned with in this world, in your own right, and Queen, I salute you.

Prayer

Father, I ask that You open the eyes of my understanding. Allow me to see the power that You have granted me in the kingdom. Allow me to acknowledge the authority that I carry as Your daughter. I thank You for thinking enough of me while I was in my mother's womb to make me a woman. Let me not be ashamed nor allow myself to feel belittled or undervalued because of how You chose to make me. I recognize that You do everything on purpose and that You make no mistakes. I thank You for giving me the confidence, strength and understanding I need to be the woman of God You have always wanted me to be. Help me to see myself the way that You see me. Reveal to me the unique and magnificent calling and purpose that You have placed on my life for such a time as this. I thank You for fearfully and wonderfully making me just as I am, and I thank You for pushing me to a higher calling than where I currently am. I thank You for giving me the wisdom I need to positively influence the people around me, for helping me to walk boldly and confidently in the authority You have given me, and for gifting me with the grace to operate in the Power I inherited from You by being Your child. I love You and thank You for all of these things.

In Jesus's name, Amen.

Just in Case You Forgot

♥ You were chosen before the foundation of the world to be *exactly who you are*! (Ephesians 1:4)

♥ You are a product of the skillful hand of the Master and you were created for the purpose of good works, not evil desires. (Ephesians 2:10)

♥ You are fashioned in your Father's image, so you cannot be lowly, undervalued, or insignificant, because your Father is none of those things. (Genesis 1:27)

♥ You are fearfully and wonderfully made. And while this is not all that you are, it is important for you to never forget that you *are* beautiful in every way. (Psalm 139:14)

♥ You are a powerful believer who can do mighty things in the kingdom. (Mark 16:17-18)

♥ You were formed intentionally by God and called for a great purpose. (Jeremiah 1:5)

Notes

Let the Process Begin

Esther 2:12 NLT. ¹² *Before each young woman was taken to the King's bed, she was given the prescribed twelve months of beauty treatments—six months with oil of myrrh, followed by six months with special perfumes and ointments.*

Chapter 2 Breakdown

Let the search begin! After Queen Vashti's act of defiance, the King decided that she would no longer be Queen. And, in an effort to find her replacement, King Ahasuerus commanded that all of the fair virgins throughout his entire kingdom be brought to his palace in Susa. Hadassah, our heroine, was among the women who were taken to the palace. However, Hadassah would now be referred to as Esther because her cousin and guardian, Mordecai, warned her to keep her Jewish heritage a secret. Now, after the women were gathered, they were each required to undergo a yearlong purification process, with herbs and spices. It was during this process that Esther was able to gain favor, above all the other women, amongst the officers and the eunuchs. After the yearlong process was complete, each woman was allowed to have one night to meet with the King. If the King liked the woman and called her by name, she would be allowed to return to the King's chambers; if not, she would join the harem. When it was Esther's turn to meet with the King, he immediately fell in love with her. Esther had found favor with the King and subsequently became Queen.

There is a period of transition that will shift you from your now to your next. This period is called "process". And in order to become Queen, *you must endure the process.*

Now, before I took the time to really look at this chapter, I had always assumed that Esther's journey to the throne was a relatively short one. You know, she gets chosen to go to the palace, puts on a nice dress, the King immediately falls in love with her, then *boom*, Esther is the Queen! However, her process was not that simple.

You see, after the women were brought to the palace, they had to go through an entire year's worth of pampering and prepping before they could even stand in the King's presence. The Bible tells us that each woman was required to go before the King one at a time. So, let's do the math. Let's assume that 20 young women were chosen from each of the 127 provinces in the kingdom. That's a little over 2,500 women that the King would have to meet. If the King met with one woman each day, it would have taken him close to 7 years to meet every young woman that was taken the palace. Now, the Bible tells us that Esther went before the King in the tenth month of the seventh year of his reign. Remember, the King threw his feast that we talked about in the previous chapter in the third year of his reign. That means it took a little over four years for Esther to finally get an audience with the King!

So, what am I saying to you? God has so much in store for you, but you cannot skip ahead of the process and go straight to purpose. And get this, your process may take a while! The process is the key that unlocks the door to purpose; it is not optional. Why? Because if you do not allow yourself to endure the process now, you will mismanage your purpose later!

Think about it! At the time that Hadassah was taken off of the streets of Susa and brought into the palace, she knew *nothing* about being a Queen. Furthermore, she probably would have messed up her meeting with the King had she not gone through the proper steps and taken the time to adequately prepare herself.

Same with you! Think about all of the lessons that life has taught you. Think about how you were taught to speak, stand, and walk in the company of others. Think about how your life experiences have shaped the way that you view other people. Think about how you view yourself. Now don't get me wrong, there are some things that you have learned that were necessary for your survival and your growth during a previous season in your life. However, there are some survival tactics, some relationships, and some defense mechanisms that you developed while living as a captive in the streets of Susa that will hinder you from being Queen if you bring them to the palace. In other words, what you learned back then may sustain you now, but it will not take you forward! This is why one of the most challenging aspects of the process is recognizing that you have a lot to unlearn.

Let's get real for a second. Everything that you have learned and every person you have become connected to, cannot follow you into your next season. Notice that Esther went into the palace alone! Now, I am not saying that everything that you learned on the streets of your Susa was bad. You learned how to survive, you learned how to persevere, and you learned how to be strong for everyone around you, which is great. But now you are moving into the palace. And while you did learn some great things on the outside, somewhere along the way, you picked up some attitudes, bad habits, ungodly relationships, and insecurities that have to be uprooted before you can walk fully into your calling.

Truth be told, some of you are in the midst of your process right now! God has been reshaping and remaking you and you have felt conflicted, uncomfortable, and challenged more than ever before. You have no idea what God is doing in your life, where you are going, and some of you don't even know who you are becoming. The journey has been a difficult and lonely one for you. On the other hand, some of you have not started your process yet. The interesting thing is, you have not started your process not because God hasn't called you to it yet; but because you have become so familiar with brokenness, hurt, and being "tough", that the idea of being stripped of what is now comfortable for you, intimidates you. You're running from purpose because you actually believe that your brokenness is a part of who you are.

But I want to encourage you, my Sister, regardless as to whatever stage you are currently in, the fact still remains that the process is necessary! To the woman currently in the middle of process, keep moving forward. I know that the prepping and the breaking is never fun, but what a glorious unfolding it shall be, when God gets through molding you and gives you a new name. And to my Sister who has not yet found the courage to begin her process, don't refuse to say "yes" to God because you're afraid of change! Let God have His way and let Him make you whole! Wherever you currently are in your walk with God, be encouraged! For in this season, God is saying, "I am isolating you and pulling things out of you, not to punish you and not because you did anything wrong, but because I have more for you!"

I know that the unlearning and relearning process can be daunting, and I understand that this road can be a lonely one sometimes. But I promise you, it will all be worth it!

Now we have talked about process, but there is one more interesting part of this passage of scripture that we must discuss. The Bible tells us that while Esther was going through her process, Mordecai passed by the gate of the palace *everyday* to check on her.

Why is this important? It is imperative that while you are going through process, you always remember that you are not alone! Just because you are in an unfamiliar place with unfamiliar people does not mean that you have been forsaken. Because, just like Esther, while you are steadily going through your process, your Father above is passing by the gate of your place of transition, watching over you every step of the way! So be encouraged and know that the process may be difficult, but the Father is watching over you.

So, my Sister, endure, press on, and never stop striving to become the Queen you were always destined to be. You are not alone. You can do this, and your time is right now!

Prayer

Father, I submit to the process! Whatever is not like You, that resides within me, I ask You to remove it now in Jesus's name. I understand that the process may not happen as fast as I would like it to, so I ask that You give me the patience to endure it. Though it may hurt and while it may be uncomfortable, I know that it is all for my good. I want to be used and I want to be right with You. I thank You for thinking enough of me to choose me to go through the process so that I may be better equipped to do Your will. While I am still on this journey, please give me the strength, grace, and confidence necessary to carry on. Help me to not get weary and please don't let me move out of turn or out of season. God, make me whole. I give You complete control over my life. God, remind me, that You are with me and that this is not a punishment for me. Hold my hand and walk with me every step of the way. Speak encouraging words to me and let me not compare my journey to my sister's. Help me to focus on the path You have set before me. Father, I thank You in advance for all of the great blessings and miracles that shall befall me after my training season is over!

In Jesus's name, Amen.

Just in Case You Forgot

♥ You are now challenged to seek things that are above; not things that are comfortable or familiar. (Colossians 3:1)

♥ You are now required to change your thinking. (Philippians 4:8)

♥ You are pressing towards a higher calling. (Philippians 3:14)

♥ You are not alone. (Deuteronomy 31:6); (Hebrews 13:5); (Matthew 28:20)

♥ You will get through this with the help of the Lord. (Philippians 4:13)

♥ What you are experiencing right now, cannot even be compared to what God is about to do in your life. (Romans 8:18)

Notes

Dealing with Haman

Esther 3:1 NLT. Some time later, King Xerxes promoted Haman son of Hammedatha the Agagite over all the other nobles, making him the most powerful official in the empire.

Chapter 3 Breakdown

Haman, the Agagite and villain in this story, was appointed as a nobleman in the King's court. Because Haman was a nobleman, other subjects in the kingdom were required to bow down before him as a sign of respect. One day, as Haman was passing by, Mordecai refused to bow down to him. This enraged Haman so much that he went to the King and told him that Mordecai's people, the Jews, were disobedient to the King's laws and that the King should not let them live. Being deceived, not to mention, completely unaware of the fact that Esther was a Jew, the King agreed that the Jews should be utterly destroyed. Therefore, Haman, operating under the King's authority, set a decree in the land stating that on the 13th day of the 12th month of the year, all of the Jews in the King's kingdom would be massacred.

There is one thing that holds women back from pursuing purpose more than anything else, *the past*!

Now what exactly does this passage of scripture have to do with the past? I'll show you.

In 1 Samuel Chapter 15, we encounter Samuel (the prophet to the Israelites) and Saul (the King of the Israelites). Now, in those times, the prophet would hear from God and relay what God was saying about the people to the King. At this particular moment in history, the Lord commanded Saul to destroy all of the Amalekite people along with all of their property (goats, sheep, cows, *everything*) as punishment for how they preyed upon the Israelites when they came out of captivity in Egypt. While Saul did set out to destroy the Amalekite people, he disobeyed God by sparing many of the animals in the Amalekite camp and the King of the Amalekites, whose name was Agag.

Now, in Esther Chapter 3 verse 1, the Bible says that Haman was an Agagite. Usually in scripture, the suffix –ite denotes the descendants of a particular person or group of people (i.e. Israelites = descendants of Israel). While Agag was later killed by the prophet Samuel, here we find an Agagite (descendant of Agag) several years later who has a huge vendetta against the Jews. Ironic, huh?

Isn't it amazing how, when we don't handle the issues of our past when we have the opportunity to, they come back and wreak more havoc in our lives than we could have ever imagined? And get this, sometimes they don't even wreak havoc in our lives directly. No, sometimes they go straight to the next generation and start trying to attack our children and grandchildren! Remember, Saul is the one who disobeyed God, not Esther and not Mordecai. Yet, here we are decades later, dealing with the consequences of Saul's actions.

Listen, it's scary and it's not fun and sometimes, it's not even our fault. But my Sister, you must understand that you cannot become Esther without confronting Hadassah. For it is only after you have dealt with your past *properly*, that you can you walk into your Queendom *confidently*.

And let me share this super deep revelation with you really quick; *everybody has a past*. The End. Somebody send me an offering! But in all seriousness. I do not care who you are or how holy you look! Everyone has *something* in their past that they need to deal with. And choosing not to deal with your past is dangerous business. Don't get me wrong, there is power in the blood of Jesus and yes, once you accept Him as your Lord and Savior, your past sins are wiped off of your record and you are no longer bound to sin. However, just because your sins are covered does not mean that you don't have to deal with the ramifications of those sins.

Unpopular Opinion Alert: You can be saved and not delivered from your past! Salvation and deliverance are two completely different processes. Salvation happens when we let God be the Lord over our *souls*. Deliverance happens when we let God be the Lord over our *issues*. There are too many women who have been saved by grace that are still bound by their pasts. But now is the time to go to God and get free.

What am I saying? You've prayed about it and you've been saved from it. That's great! Now go deal with it. *Handle it before it handles you*! No more sweeping things under the rug. And no more being ashamed or scared of whatever "it" is or was. You must confront it! Your future and the deliverance of the generations that are coming after you are depending on you being bold enough to face your Haman.

Confronting your past is a critical component of you being able to walk into your purpose. I don't care how long ago it happened, face it! Whether it is the unforgiveness of a parent; bitterness about a failed relationship; the loss of a loved one that you have yet to recover from; low self-esteem due to verbal abuse and bullying; heartbreak; addictions to sex, pornography or drugs/alcohol; a promiscuous past; experiences with sexual abuse; pathological and habitual lying, cheating; experiences with domestic violence or mental abuse; suicidal thoughts and depression; or bad attitudes... I mean, the list goes on and on and on! I don't care what mistake you made that you keep beating yourself up about, or what happened to you in your past, give it to God today so that it won't keep you from your destiny tomorrow! And don't be fooled, just because you don't talk about it, doesn't mean it doesn't still have a hold on you.

My Sister, your secrets can be deadly and, trust me, if the enemy cannot take you out with those secret struggles, the next generation is on his hit list. You may have been able to keep your depression under wraps (or so you think), but your children may not be so lucky. It's up to you to *expose and confront your demons*!

In the proceeding chapters, we will learn that it was only after Esther confronted Haman head on, that she was able to bring victory and salvation to herself and to her people. Could it be that the reason that your children and other family members cannot get free is because you have been too fearful to speak up and confront your past?

Let me encourage you, you have absolutely no reason to fear. Don't worry about what other people might say or how they might look at you after you share your testimony. How they feel does not matter! Your freedom is more important than man's opinion. And, as long as God validates you, what others have to say is completely irrelevant. You have to realize that your past is only a reflection of where you've been, not who you are! You may have fallen, made mistakes, or even been through hell and back. But now is the time for you to leave that old girl in the past and walk with your head held high, knowing that your Father has already covered it all under His blood and given you the strength to face it without fear of condemnation.

The enemy loves to remind us of our mistakes, dig up old dirt when things are going well, and tell us who we were and how we used to behave. He is the king of re runs, but it's time for you to learn how to change the channel. Don't let the enemy convince you (and don't you convince yourself) that because of where you've been, you don't deserve what God has promised you.

Now please hear my heart. I am in no way saying that you should not be allowed the time to grieve or feel pain concerning whatever has happened to you or feel sorry for what you did in your past. But, after the grieving and sorrow have gone, you must move forward. You cannot become a hostage to your past! Now is *not* the time to reminisce and put old stories on rewind. Now is *not* the time to let your past cripple you. Now is *not* the time to sweep your past under the rug. You have work to do and a generation whose deliverance is dependent upon not only your salvation but your authentic deliverance. You are no longer Hadassah; you *are* Queen Esther and it's high time for you to move on.

God wants to heal the hurting and dark places of your suffering. He wants to help you work towards forgiving yourself as He has already forgiven you. I encourage you to do whatever is necessary to get deliverance: fast, pray, even seek professional counseling if you think it will help. But you have to do something.

Your past has as much power over you as you let it. You can continue to fear your Haman, or you can *fight* him. The choice is yours.

Prayer

Father, thank You for the forgiving and redeeming power of Your blood. Thank You for dying on a cross just for me so that I could live a life free from sin and free from the torment of my past. I thank You for saving me and washing my sins away. And if I am not yet saved, I ask that You grant me the revelation of your Son Jesus Christ, so that I may know You on a different level. Now God, I need Your strength more than ever before. Lord, my Haman is trying to haunt me, and I need You to help me overcome him. I know, and I recognize that I cannot do this by myself. Father, I need you! I request forgiveness for what it is that I have done or held on to. And I ask You to forgive me for not dealing with my past sooner. But I am asking that complete and authentic deliverance overtake me now in Jesus's name. And, I ask that You will allow the same grace and peace that you have given me, to pass on to my children and other family members who are dealing with the same issues as I am. Now, Father, I ask that You help me to forgive myself. I need to see myself *exactly* how You see me. When dark times come, and bad memories start to resurface, let me not be anxious, but God, remind me of how much you love me. Thank you for loving me. Thank you for keeping me. Thank you for forgiving me. And thank you for helping me to overcome my past and walk boldly into my future.

In Jesus's name, Amen.

Just in Case You Forgot

♥ You are *not* who you used to be nor are you bound by what you have done! You *are* a new creature in Jesus Christ and the past is gone! (2 Corinthians 5:17)

♥ You are redeemed, and your sins have been swept away. (Isaiah 44:22)

♥ Your Sins have been *forgiven* and *forgotten...* now forgive yourself. (Isaiah 43:25)

♥ You have been covered by the Father's mercy. (Daniel 9:9)

♥ You are the righteousness of God. (2 Corinthians 5:21)

♥ There is nothing you have done that the love of God cannot cover. (1 Peter 4:8)

♥ Regardless of what you have done or the road you have traveled, you are incapable of being separated from the love of God. (Romans 8:31-38)

♥ You have to be proactive about getting your deliverance and keeping your freedom. Stay in God's face! (Matthew 17:21) (Mark 9:29)

Notes

Just Say Yes

Esther 4: 14-16 NLT. ¹⁴ *If you keep quiet at a time like this, deliverance and relief for the Jews will arise from some other place, but you and your relatives will die. Who knows if perhaps you were made Queen for just such a time as this?"* ¹⁵ *Then Esther sent this reply to Mordecai:* ¹⁶ *"Go and gather together all the Jews of Susa and fast for me. Do not eat or drink for three days, night or day. My maids and I will do the same. And then, though it is against the law, I will go in to see the king. If I must die, I must die."*

Chapter 4 Breakdown

In this chapter, the Jewish people are mourning, weeping and fasting because they have just received word of Haman's new law. In desperate need of help, Mordecai goes to Esther and asks her to go before the King and beg him for mercy on behalf of the people. But, Esther explains to Mordecai that going before the King in the inner court without an invitation is an unlawful act that is punishable by death. Mordecai then tells Esther that if she does not go before the King, help would come from another place for everyone except for her. Knowing this, Esther asks that the people join together in prayer and fasting with her as she decides to go before the King even though it could cost her her life.

"Who knows if perhaps you were made Queen for such a time as this?" Esther 4:14. There is nothing about you that was a coincidence. The era you were born in, your complexion, your height, your build, your laugh, your smile, the family you were born into, your experiences (both good and bad), the job you work, your passions and hobbies. *Nothing* was on accident. You, yes *you* (with all of your flaws, quirks and shortcomings), were called for such a time as this. But you were not just called so that you could be excited about being called. The calling on your life has far more to do with helping someone else than with making yourself great. Your commitment to walking in your Queenly authority is not just for your own benefit. There is a generation whose survival is dependent upon your "Yes, Lord, *I will go.*"

Looking at the scriptures above, we recognize that there was no other woman on Earth who could do what Esther was called to do. "But Ariona, I thought that the scripture said that if she did not go, the Jews deliverance would come from a different place?" You're right! But take note, while the Bible did say that deliverance would come from "a different place" it did not say that someone else would be able to take Esther's place. What does that mean? No one could do what God told Esther to do, the *way* God told her to do it, except for Esther! Vashti could not have done it. The other women in the harem could

48

not have done do it. And Mordecai could not have done it. No, this one had to be done by Esther, exactly how God asked her to do it. What am I saying to you? *You cannot pass off your gifts, your callings or your assignments on to other people!* If God wanted them to do it, He would have asked them. But He asked you on purpose! No one can do what God called you to do, the way God called you to do it, except for you.

"But Ariona, I am terrified." So was Esther! Esther's actions could have cost her her very life! Now, you may not be fearful that your actual life may be in danger, but maybe you are afraid of what your social or personal life will look like once you give God that "Yes". Maybe you are afraid of the level of responsibility that will be required of you once you give God a "Yes". Maybe you're tired of giving God your "Yes" because you're tired of being different from everyone else (this was me). But let me be clear, your "No" to God does not save you.

God wants to use you, but please understand this, He will not force you. He is the Ultimate Gentleman, so following Him will *always* be a decision that you will have to make. But be very clear, your "No" only benefits your flesh for the moment. Your "No", because of whatever excuse you are making (because it is just that, an excuse), will keep you from living at your fullest potential in this life. And don't be deceived, just because things may look good right now when you tell God "No" does not mean you're off the hook; know that your "no" comes at a price. You can have money and give God a "No". You can have cars and give God a "No". But one thing that you will be lacking once you give God a "No" is peace. My Sister, make it a point to leave this Earth having held nothing back and leaving no stone unturned! It's been driving you nuts anyways, you might as well just say "Yes". You keep feeling this undeniable pull towards greater, but you've been so afraid to step out on faith that you refuse to go. But you cannot stay here any longer! It's time for you to experience more!

And I can hear you now, "I mean it's not that big of a deal. Who is really going to be affected by my 'No'. I'm just one person." Wrong! Remember, in the first chapter we learned that your power, authority and influence, reach beyond cultural, economic, religious and geographical barriers. Your "Yes" could save millions because you have the power to reach millions. Not only that, but wasn't our Savior born through the lineage of the Jews. So, hypothetically speaking, if Esther said "No" and all of the Jews were murdered (and the Father decided not to intervene), wouldn't we be left Savior-less? So, could it not be said that, Esther's "Yes, I will go" helped save all of us some thousands of years later from eternal punishment? Still think your "yes" is not important? Your "yes" is a ripple effect and you have no idea the impact that one simple act of obedience can have on the lives of not only the people around you, but the many generations after you!

I encourage you, even though you may be afraid, give God that "Yes"! Do it exactly how God said to do it! Because being used by God will be one of the most rewarding experiences of your entire life. Trust me, I know that it is a heavy burden, but He would never have asked you to do it, if He did not know that you were strong enough to handle it! God is with you every step of the way.

Now, shake the dust of your feet, get your mind off of yourself, and go walk in your calling. We're waiting on you! Because if you don't do it, it will never get done.

Prayer

Father forgive me for being selfish. Forgive me for being so consumed with my own desires and ambitions that I considered what You have for me to do as not being important. Father, redeem the time that I have wasted going back and forth about giving you a complete "YES". Please, help me not to be afraid of my own purpose. Help me to realize that You have already given me the strength to do what You are asking me to do. Help me to not be afraid of other people's opinions or this new sense of responsibility. But help me to remember that You are the captain of my soul. God, I give You my life, therefore it is Yours to do as You see fit. I am Your vessel, now help me to align my will with Yours and to walk boldly into my calling. Never let me forget that everything I do is for Your glory and not for my personal benefit. Help me not to be self-seeking in this season. But help me to remember that I am, first, called to be a servant; a servant to You and a servant to Your people. I am Your hands and feet God, and I will go if You go with me! I submit my will. I am Yours. Use me for Your glory.

In Jesus's name, Amen.

Just in Case You Forgot

♥ You are obligated to serve only one Master. You must choose daily which Master you will serve. (Matthew 6:24)

♥ God honors you when you serve Him. (John 12:26)

♥ You have been called to do greater things as a reward for being faithful over few things, not as a punishment. (Matthew 25:21)

♥ You must submit your will to the Father's; without submission there is no manifestation. (Luke 22:42)

♥ Your obedience is better than your sacrifice. (1 Samuel 15:22)

♥ You are not God, so stop trying to figure out why He picked you to do it, just do it. (Isaiah 55:8)

♥ Somebody is waiting on your "Yes, Lord, I will Go!" (Romans 8:19)

Notes

Put on Your Royal Garments

Esther 5:1 NLT. On the third day of the fast, Esther put on her royal robes and entered the inner court of the palace, just across from the King's hall. The King was sitting on his royal throne, facing the entrance.

Chapter 5 Breakdown

In this Chapter, Esther gathered up enough courage, with the help of the Lord, to go before the King. She has prayed, she has fasted, and now she is ready to go. Esther puts on her royal garments and walks into the inner court. When the King saw her in the court, he showed her favor. And even though she had just broken the law, he told her told that whatever she desired would be given to her, even if she asked for half of the kingdom! Queen Esther then invited both Haman and the King to dine with her on two separate occasions so that she could eventually reveal Haman's plot to destroy the Jews (she asked twice because the first time she didn't tell the King about Haman's plot).

I played softball all throughout high school and the team that I played on was not a very large one, so every player was extremely valuable. And like any other sports teams, we had to wear uniforms. Our uniforms consisted of our jerseys, black pants, sliding pad, maroon and gold socks, maroon belt, our cleats and, our catching glove. While there were some items that were smaller than others, each item was essential for us to be able to play the game effectively. The uniform symbolized both our connection to the school and to each other. Furthermore, it let the umpires know that we were ready to play.

Now, let's get spiritual for a second. You are a Queen and you have authority! Yes, we know! But if you do not have on the right apparel, how will anyone else ever know that? Furthermore, how will anyone know who you are connected to, if you always show up to the game with the wrong uniform on. In other words, how do you expect people to know that you are a Christian and there's nothing about you that demonstrates that you belong to Christ?

Think about it, if Esther had on the clothes that she wore when she first came into the palace, do you think the guards would have let her come into the inner court. No, they would have thought she was a common woman and turned her away. But she wore her royal garment as a sign of authority and power and to let them know who she was!

After you have accepted the fact that you are a Queen, you must make the decision to behave and dress accordingly. Now just to clarify, I am not talking about your actual physical clothes; this is not that kind of party. No, I am talking about your spirit woman. Stay with me! Just like every team member has a uniform, every Queen has things that she carries with her that let the outside world know who she is.

So, what exactly are your royal garments? Well, as a Christian, your garments consist of many things, including the full armor of God as well as the fruits of the Spirit. I like to think of the armor of God (things people may not physically see) as your foundational garments and the fruits of the Spirit (things people will see through your behavior) as the things that will continue to get added to you over time like a royal robe, scepter, crown, etc.

Now, what is the armor of God? Glad you asked! It consists of several items, all of which are described in Ephesians 6:10-17. The armor of God includes: the helmet of salvation, the sword of the spirit, the belt of truth, the breastplate of righteousness, the shield of faith, and your feet prepared with peace. These items are necessary for every Queen. The armor of God not only prepares you for battle, but it also helps solidify your identity and faith in Christ.

I'll briefly break down what the purpose of each of these pieces of armor is and why they are so significant.

1. The Helmet of Salvation: I like to think of this as surety and confidence in your place in God. You have to *know* not only that you are saved but you must also be sure of who you are and who God has called you to be. Your identity must be solidified in Christ because the enemy likes to pick fights on the battlefields of our minds. Given that fact, it is

imperative that you remind yourself daily who you are and more importantly, *Whose* you are!

2. The Sword of the Spirit: This is the word of God. It is so important for you to be reading your word. You must be able to use the word of God as a weapon against any of the enemy's tricks. The Bible is your ultimate weapon. Cherish it, study it and commit as much of it as possible to memory. Because when the enemy comes against you, the only thing that is strong enough to defeat him is the word of God.

3. The Belt of Truth: The Bible specifically says, "gird up your loins with truth". The loins are the sexual organs in the body and in order to increase mobility, before a fight, the men would "gird up their loins" by taking the bottom halves of their robes or tunics and tying them through their legs and around their waists (the end result would look somewhat like shorts). So essentially, the phrase "gird up your loins" simply means "prepare to fight". This phrase can mean several things for you. Not only must you prepare yourself to fight, but you must cover yourself in the truth. The enemy is the king of lies, so everyday you must be prepared to combat what he says that you are with who God says that you are! Also, know that what you cover yourself with, determines what you birth out. What do I mean? Completely immersing yourself in the truth (what God has promised and spoken over you) will affect what comes out of you. If you allow yourself to accept the lies of the enemy, what God

has promised you will not be able to manifest or be birthed out of you. You must learn to, daily remind yourself of and stand on God's promises, no matter what the enemy throws your way.

4. The Breastplate of Righteousness: The purpose of a breastplate is to protect and cover the heart and the vital organs. Proverbs 4:23 implores us to guard our hearts with diligence because out of it flow the issues of life. We do not follow our hearts, we follow Christ! Furthermore, the Bible tells us that we need to guard our hearts. Maybe this explains why some of us have encountered so much chaos over the years, because we have been following after what we were supposed to be keeping close watch over. Bottom line, your heart is precious, it is important, and it can be tricky. Cover your heart, your motives, and your intentions with the righteousness of God so that you will not be able to be lead astray!

5. The Shield of Faith: What does a shield do? It is used to block strikes from the opposition and, sometimes, it is used to push your opponent back as you advance forward. Your faith in God keeps you moving forward and keeps the enemy at bay. Do not be discouraged by whatever the enemy has thrown at you. Just keep fighting because great mountains have been moved with little faith.

6. Your Feet Prepared with Peace: Walk in peace! You have got to learn to carry peace with you, daily. God promised Joshua in Joshua 1:3, that every place that the sole of his foot touched, the Lord had

already given him. Walk in victory and in peace knowing that wherever you go God has already been and you have already won the victory!

These 6 items are integral parts of your daily wardrobe! But that's not all that you will have to worry about wearing.

Along with the armor of God, every saint must add to their royal garments the fruits of the spirit (Galatians 5:22-23). As royalty and as heirs to the kingdom, naturally you gain an inheritance from your Father. These inheritances do not just affect your level of authority and power, but for true daughters of the King, they should begin to reveal themselves in your character. Your Queenly robe, your crown, your scepter are represented in the fruit that you bear. Love, joy, peace, patience, kindness, goodness, faithfulness, gentleness and self control are a part of the royal garments that you must learn to wear and they will continue to be added to your "apparel" as you grow in God.

Now, before this chapter ends, I want to bring your attention to one last thing. When Esther came before the King in her royal garb, notice that the King told her that whatever she wanted she could have; even if it was half of the kingdom. Whoa! Now remember, the King's kingdom encompassed 127 provinces stretching from India to Ethiopia. That's about 63 provinces that he was willing to hand over to Esther, right after she blatantly disobeyed the law!

Why is this important? Your acceptance of the call of God over your life and your decision to wear the royal garments listed above will grant you access to blessings that you have never seen before. Moreover, the reason that you have not seen the hand of God in your life yet is because you have not been walking like the Queen that you were destined to be. God has blessings laid up in heaven that are waiting on you. But if in your daily life you do not resemble the royalty that you claim to be, you will miss out.

All God has been requiring you to do is accept the Queenly mantle that He has predestined for you to carry. Once you adorn yourself in your royal garments and begin to exude the character of a Queen, trust me when I tell you that miracles, blessings and a brand-new level of access will overtake you. Your advancement in the kingdom is tied to your acceptance of the call. So, Queen, dust off that crown, put on your royal garments and walk forward into destiny!!

Prayer

Father let me never forget that You have called me to exude the character of royalty. Let me never forget that as a daughter of the King of Kings, I have a right to an inheritance far beyond my wildest dreams. Help me to begin to bear the fruits of the spirit. I want to represent you well God. Remind me to daily, put on full armor of God so that I can withstand any attacks from the enemy. Let me not wear my royal garments for my own praise and adoration but let everything that I do be for Your glory! God, I want to be the Queen that You ordained me to be before the foundation of the Earth. I accept the call, I put on my mantle and I thank You in advance for doors that You have already opened because of my yes!

In Jesus's name, Amen.

Just in Case You Forgot

♥ You are royalty! (1 Peter 2:9)
♥ You are not a Queen based on how you look but based on who you are and how you act! (1 Peter 3:3-4)
♥ You are a fighter first! (Ephesians 6:13-17)
♥ You are already victorious! (Joshua 1:3)
♥ You must towards mastering the fruits of the spirit! They remind the people around you who you belong to! (Galatians 5:22-23).

Notes

Focus on Your Own Table

Esther 6:14 NLT. While they were still talking, the king's eunuchs arrived and quickly took Haman to the banquet Esther had prepared.

Chapter 6 Breakdown

Now the King became restless one night and had the records of the chronicles, which are almost like daily minutes, read to him. In the records of the chronicles, it was written that Mordecai had saved the King's life by exposing two men who were plotting to kill the King. Because of Mordecai's actions, the King wanted to honor Mordecai, but he had no idea how. Now Haman was approaching the King that same night to ask if he could hang Mordecai on the gallows he had personally built for him in his own back yard. But before Haman could ask for Mordecai's life, the King asked Haman how he should honor a man whom he cherished. Haman, thinking that the King was talking about him, listed all of these elaborate things that the King should do to honor such a man. The King then required Haman to do all of those elaborate things not for himself, but for Mordecai. While all of this was happening, Esther was busy preparing a banquet for Haman and the King.

Distractions bring death to purpose. There are so many things going on in this chapter between the King, Haman and Mordecai, but in the text, Esther is steady preparing the banquet for Haman and the King. Had Esther allowed herself to become consumed with the fact that the King found favor in her and spared her life or had she started to worry about Mordecai, she would have missed her opportunity to prepare her table.

Your table is your assignment. God has put a "table" in front of each of us that we must prepare. That table is where we do our fighting and our infiltrating of the kingdom of darkness. There is a territory that only *your* hands can prepare a table in. The maidservants could not prepare this table, her best friends could not prepare this table. No, this was Esther's fight, Esther's call, and Esther's table to prepare and she buckled down, stayed focused and did what she was called to do.

But here is where the problem lies. Sometimes, we can get so infatuated with the call that we forget to do the work. As my First Lady put it in a previous sermon, "don't get stuck in the last move!" Don't let your victory, your progress, or even sympathy for other people's dilemmas distract you from purpose!

This chapter is primarily about what Mordecai and Haman are doing. And while they did have a lot of issues going on, Esther never stopped what she was doing to involve herself in Mordecai's business. At no time does the scripture say that Esther tried to console Mordecai about the enemy he was facing, or that she tried to go to the King on Mordecai's behalf. Rather, Esther stayed focused on *her* own assignment, even though there was turmoil going on all around her.

My Sister, do yourself a favor and get focused like Esther! Do not sacrifice the time that God has given you to prepare your own table, trying to help someone else with theirs. As women, sometimes we possess the "Superwoman" spirit. But you cannot save everybody. When people have issues, when someone is going through hard times, when our friends and family just need somebody to talk to, some of us tend to drop whatever we are doing to help them. Now, I am not telling you not to be helpful, kind, generous or even empathetic to others. But, I am telling you to use wisdom. Because right now, your time is very precious and cannot be wasted doing anything other than pursuing purpose.

The funny thing is, while you have been reading this, you already have someone in mind that you know is a time waster and a drama attractor. We all know that one person who never has anything going right in their lives, *ever.* The one who always has some drama-filled catastrophe that they have to tell you about that is everyone else's fault but theirs. You know, those people who have drama and chaos just fall out of the sky... in their laps... every week (I hope you can sense my side eye). Or maybe you are familiar with the one who calls you only to dump all that they are dealing with on you without even asking if you are doing okay. Or my personal favorites, the one who, no matter how many times they cry, no matter how many times you talk to them, and no matter how much advice you give them, they always ends up right back in the thick of it. Listen!!

In this season, you have got to prioritize yourself, your peace and your calling over other people's drama. Because the reality of the situation is this, *you are not their God!* And I guarantee that whatever they are dealing with can be better handled by Him than you. "But they need me." No, they need God; some of you just need other people to need you. "But I feel bad if I don't help." Anyone who is guilt tripping you or manipulating you into being there for them does not have your best interest at heart in the first place. Buckle down and stop using other people as an excuse as to why you haven't done what God has called you to do. *It is time for you to focus on your own table!* This opportunity may not come around again. So, it's now or never.

Sometimes it's not even friends that distract us. Sometimes it is our families. And Lord knows I understand how difficult it can be to balance your personal goals with family. But you have got to pray and ask God for wisdom because sometimes you just have to say, "I love you but I have got to focus" and let God handle the rest.

And then there are those of you hopeful romantics who have slowed down your process or even changed your course completely for a man. My beloved Sister (when you add the beloved you know it's about to get real), listen to me, if it is meant to be, it will be, but in the meantime, *there is work that needs to be done.* And here's a hint for you, the right man will pull you closer to purpose, not farther away from it! And if he's drawing you away from purpose, I can tell you now, that's not the right one. A true man of God understands the importance of operating in the timing of God and being obedient to His instructions. He will also understand that your primary focus before marriage is God, not him. Moral of the story, he'll still be there if it's God's will; now *get back to work*!!

There are some things that God has put in your hands to complete, but you have been so distracted by toxic relationships that you have neglected your own table. Your table could be full time ministry or med school. Your table could be owning your own salon or a podcast. Your table could be writing your own book or starting a business. Whatever your table is, go and prepare it! The work will never get done if you don't do it. It is ok to be selfish in this season! Go hard after God! Do not forfeit your purpose, your dreams and your goals to deal with someone else's drama. Pray for them and get back to work! Time is moving on my Sister and it's time for you to move on too.

Prayer

Father, right now, I am asking You to bestow upon me divine focus. Eliminate every distraction in my life that would try to keep me from doing Your will. Help me not to feel guilty or manipulated by people who feel that they have a monopoly over my time and attention. Cut down every ungodly relationship and soul tie in my life. Help me to seek You with my whole heart! Lord I need to be able to discern the difference between a ministry opportunity and a distraction in disguise. Speak to me! Help me to help who I am supposed to help in this season and protect me from unnecessary, drama filled situationships. Forgive me for wasting my time on things that were not a priority, and things that I was never called to be a part of in the first place. Help me to be a good steward over my time and resources. And show me exactly what it is that You would have for me to do in this season!

In Jesus's name, Amen.

Just in Case You Forgot

♥ You have to keep moving forward! (Proverbs 4:25)
♥ You have to be diligent, no more procrastination, *get it done*! (Proverbs 13:4)
♥ You have to be immovable. Do not worry, your labor is not in vain, keep moving forward! (1 Corinthians 15:58)
♥ You will lose friends chasing after God, it's ok. Just like the wheat and the tare, a time of separation will come. Don't you be manipulated or made to feel guilty for doing God's will. Shake the dust off of your feet and keep on trucking! God's got you, my Sister. You are never alone. (Matthew 13:24-30)

Notes

_____

_____

_____

_____

_____

_____

_____

_____

_____

_____

_____

The Face Off With Fear

Esther 7:3-6 NLT. *³ Queen Esther replied, "If I have found favor with the King, and if it pleases the King to grant my request, I ask that my life and the lives of my people will be spared. ⁴ For my people and I have been sold to those who would kill, slaughter, and annihilate us. If we had merely been sold as slaves, I could remain quiet, for that would be too trivial a matter to warrant disturbing the King." ⁵ "Who would do such a thing?" King Xerxes demanded. "Who would be so presumptuous as to touch you?" ⁶ Esther replied, "This wicked Haman is our adversary and our enemy." Haman grew pale with fright before the King and Queen.*

Chapter 7 Breakdown

Now here is the moment we have all been waiting for; the face off between Esther and Haman. At the banquet that Esther prepared, the King told Esther again, that he would give her whatever she desired; even if she asked for half of the kingdom. It is after this that Esther asks for the salvation of her people and then reveals Haman's plot to kill all of the Jews. The King was enraged by this information and left the banquet. While the King was gone, Haman got on the bed where Esther sat and began to plead for his life. But, when the

King returned and saw Haman on the bed with his Queen, he was angered even more. As the guards seized Haman, one of the chamberlains informed the King that Haman had prepared gallows in his backyard to hang Mordecai on. Per the King's command, Haman would later be hung on those same gallows.

There is not a single doubt in my mind that Esther was afraid to tell the King about Haman's plot, especially since Haman was sitting right in front of her at the banquet. But Esther's need to pursue purpose overshadowed her fear of Haman.

There is a common misconception amongst Christians that, in order to pursue purpose, one must relinquish all fear. But, I would like to submit to you that, more often than not, you will have to make the decision to pursue purpose and obey God *in spite of* your fears?

There are 365 scriptures in the Bible that command us not to be afraid. That is one, "fear not", for every day of the year. I believe that this was done intentionally. God provided you with a year's supply of ammunition to combat the enemy with. Why? Because He understands that fear is not so easy to get rid of.

Because fear is a natural human emotion, it is unrealistic to say that you will never experience fear ever again in your life. If someone jumps out from behind a corner and you get startled, does that mean that you don't trust God? We all know that that's ridiculous! You are human, of course there will be times when you get nervous or afraid. However, there is a difference between experiencing fear and being oppressed by fear. Fear as an experience may cause you to pause, fear as an oppressive mechanism from the enemy causes paralysis.

Many of you know exactly what I am talking about. As you are reading right now, you are thinking of an area in your life that you have put on hold because you were too afraid to move forward. My Sister, you can no longer afford to waste your time being afraid. Afraid of what other people think about you; what other people might say about you; who will and won't support you; who will talk about you; whether you will fail and even whether you will succeed. How much time have you wasted being fearful of what other people think? How much of your life have you *not* lived because of your own fear? How many times have you selfishly disobeyed the voice of God because you were afraid? And how long will you let this cycle of fear continue? No more! And if I have anything to do with it, *not for another second in Jesus's name!*

Being paralyzed by fear only lets me know that you do not really know who you are in God yet. Because when you have made your calling and election sure, as it says in 2 Peter 1:10, and when you know what God has placed in your hands, you can walk through your test with your head held high and continue to press on even when fear is staring you right in the face. Don't you know that you cannot fail with God on your side? At the end of the day, the only person you really need to be fearful of is God; no one else's opinion matters.

In order to overcome being oppressed by fear, there is only one thing that you can do; get over it and go anyway! Yea I said it, get over it and go anyway. "But Ariona you don't understand." Oh, trust me I do. I used to be an anxious, fearful wreck. Everything that I did in my life was fueled by fear. Fear influenced the way that I spoke, the way I dressed, the hairstyles I wore, my relationships, driving on the highway, the jobs and scholarships I applied for, how I sang, how I worshipped, how I ministered, you name it. I literally lived my entire life in fear. It was not until I practiced making little decisions every day to follow God and cancel out the noise of the naysayers, that I was able to overcome living a fearful life. Being oppressed by fear is a choice. And I chose to live a life focused on God, above all others. And in doing so, I have been able to be free to be my most authentic self and to pursue God's purpose for my life. I'm not saying that I don't ever struggle with fear; I just chose not to let it control my decisions anymore.

My Sister, you have to understand that the only reason that the spirit of fear tries to attach itself to you is because the enemy is afraid of your purpose. He is *terrified* that you will actually become everything that God has called you to be, so he attempts to keep you immobile by consuming your thoughts with the fear of rejection, fear of not being good enough, and fear of failure. But when God has a purpose for your life, I don't care what the enemy throws at you, he cannot win! You have no reason to be afraid! The Almighty God who made Heaven and Earth is on *your* side! Trust me, God knew exactly what He was doing when He called you and He was intentional about giving you the purpose that He gave you!

So be encouraged. Yes, it is a different territory, yes you may feel nervous and afraid sometimes, but go anyway. For the Lord your God is with you!

Prayer

Father, I thank You for freedom from the spirit of fear. Thank You for allowing me to walk in Your divine freedom and for giving me the courage to embrace who I am authentically. I thank You Lord because I no longer have to be concerned with fear of being rejected because You have already called and accepted me. Father don't let my fear overshadow my purpose. And when that spirit tries to arise again, help me to remember that You are in control and that You are on my side! I speak the boldness and the confidence of God over my life and I thank You in advance for allowing me to walk into my purpose, free from the bondage of the spirit of fear.

In Jesus's name, Amen.

Just in Case You Forgot

♥ You are covered by God because He is with you
  wherever you go! (Joshua 1:9)
♥ You have not been given the spirit of fear, but God has
  bestowed upon you Power, Love and a sound mind!
  (2 Timothy 1:7)
♥ You have been given authority to walk through dark
  and dreary places without fear because God is with you!
  (Psalm 23:4)
♥ You are not afraid because the Lord is your strength!
  (Psalm 27:1)
♥ You are confident and unafraid because even though
  trouble surrounds you, it cannot overtake you!
  (Psalm 91:5-7)

Notes

No Woman Left Behind

Esther 8:1-2 NLT. On that same day King Xerxes gave the property of Haman, the enemy of the Jews, to Queen Esther. Then Mordecai was brought before the King, for Esther had told the King how they were related. [2] The King took off his signet ring—which he had taken back from Haman—and gave it to Mordecai. And Esther appointed Mordecai to be in charge of Haman's property.

Chapter 8 Breakdown

In this chapter, the King gave Esther control over Haman's property. But rather than keeping it for herself, she gave the property to Mordecai. After this exchange, Esther asked the King to have mercy on her and her people and make a new law that would save the Jewish people. The King gave Mordecai permission to use his name and his royal seal to write a new declaration that would save all the Jews in the kingdom. In addition to all of the Jews being saved, they were also given the authority to destroy every person throughout the kingdom who had planned on participating in their demise.

The Jews are saved!!! Because of Esther's courage and her willingness to be obedient, Esther was used to save all of the Jewish people in the entire kingdom! Not only that, but the people who plotted to kill the Jews would be destroyed on the same day that the massacre of the Jews was supposed to take place. What a plot twist right!

And look at Mordecai! Because of Esther's faithfulness, Mordecai got a promotion and was able to make a proclamation on the behalf of the King. The man who was hated and targeted by Haman was blessed, promoted, and given legislative authority in the kingdom because of his connection to Esther.

I know I have said this one million times, and I will keep saying it until you get it in your spirit... My Sister, it was never about you! I know that you had to do the work, that you cried, struggled, and went through a lot just to get to where you are now. But, I have to remind you that you are where you are, not just for your own personal benefit and glory. No, your process, your fight, your experiences, were all a part of the Master's plan for your life and the lives of those who you were destined to influence.

This is where humility and selflessness become critical for the believer. Do not get to the place where God has called you to be and forget to reach back and encourage the people around you. Your experiences were never your own; they have always been designed to bless someone else. Often times we tell God that we want to be used by Him. Well what do you think you will be used to do? You are a vessel being used to bring glory to God and to bless His people.

You did not make it through the struggles of being a single parent because you did something wrong. No, you overcame so that you could encourage the next young lady to walk with her head held high and know that she can make it just like you did. You did not struggle with suicide, depression, sexual assault or low self-esteem to keep that testimony to yourself. No, your testimony is supposed to encourage someone else! Be careful not to get so consumed with "keeping your secret" that you keep your mouth shut. You have the key to someone else's breakthrough, and you are hiding it! Stand up and uplift your Sisters!

The Bible says in Revelations 12:11 that they overcame by two things, the blood of the Lamb and the word of their testimony. This means that your testimony, paired with God's redeeming and cleansing blood, is the catalyst to someone else's deliverance. My sister, your story of triumph critically impacts the outcome of your Sister's deliverance. So, speak up. What good is it to have made it over just to watch your Sister struggle right next to you? You learned how to make it, now help someone else make it. There is a blessing for your Sister lying dormant inside of you!

Now that you have won, now that the plan has worked, now that you have finally overcome, *pull somebody else up*!

My Sister, once you cross that finish line, tell someone else about it! Open your mouth and share what God has done. You could literally save someone else's life! They need you and it's time for *your* story to be heard because your silence could be deadly!

Prayer

Father never allow me to get so full of pride that I refuse to help my Sister. I understand that You brought me out, not just for my own benefit, but for the progression of the kingdom of God and for the benefit of someone else. Help me to think more selflessly and give me the desire to serve and help Your people, instead of seeking to draw the attention to myself. And help me not to be afraid of my own story! But, give me the strength to share, and the discernment to know who to share my testimony with. I know that I have gone through my own tests and trials for a purpose so please show me who I am supposed to be uplifting and ministering to.

In Jesus's name, Amen.

Just in Case You Forgot

♥ You are supposed to share your testimony because somebody needs to know that they can make it too. (Revelation 12:11)

♥ Since you have been in a low place before, do not kick your Sister when she is down. You are called to uplift your sister when she falls. (Galatians 6:1) (1 Thessalonians 5:11)

♥ You are called to love and serve your Sisters! (1Peter 4:8-10)

♥ Never speak negatively about your Sister's struggles. (Ephcsians 4:29)

♥ If your Sister is not strong enough to handle a particular situation, bear her burdens for her in prayer. (Galatians 6:2)

Notes

No One Can Take Your Shine

Esther 9:12 NLT. He [the King] called for Queen Esther. He said, "The Jews have killed 500 men in the fortress of Susa alone, as well as Haman's ten sons. If they have done that here, what has happened in the rest of the provinces? But now, what more do you want? It will be granted to you; tell me and I will do it."

Chapter 9 Breakdown

It is the day of the massacre. Remember, this is the day that was originally set for the Jews to be slaughtered, but the script has been flipped and now the Jews have begun to destroy all those who sought to do them harm. All while this is happening, Mordecai is being promoted in the kingdom and his name is becoming well known amongst the King's servants and throughout all the provinces. He and Esther even teamed up to write a decree in the kingdom. However, throughout all of this, the King still comes back to Esther and asks her again if she has any other requests. Esther asks that Haman's sons be hanged like their father, and it was done.

This part of Esther's story is very interesting. The Jews have won, all those that plotted against them have been destroyed, and Mordecai is continuing to get promoted in the kingdom; he has even become more well known amongst the people. But even in the midst of the Jews' victory and Mordecai's promotion, the King *still* managed to come back and make sure that Esther was satisfied. For the third time, the King says essentially, "Honey, is there anything else that I can do for you?" Amazing! In the midst of chaos and transitions in government, Esther still had the King's attention.

I really feel that you need this reminder, *God has not forgotten about you!* He still sees you, my Sister!

So often, we get intimidated when other people begin to be elevated, especially if it's in an area that we are operating in. And if the other person being blessed is another woman, some of us lose our sanity!

If you knew who you were in God, you would have no reason to be intimidated by anyone else's success! There is a lane that only your feet are called to walk in! And even if that lane is on the same street as another woman, remember that just because there are other women in the same field as you, doesn't mean that you weren't called to be there. Also, do not foolishly be jealous of a seed that has started to grow that you helped plant! You should not become jealous when someone that you have poured into starts to flourish; you should want to see them progress and reach a higher level than you did. No ma'am, it's all unacceptable. Where is your confidence in the love that God has for you? Have you forgotten who you are in Christ? Do you not know that you are absolutely amazing, that the favor of God is all over your life, and that *no one can steal your shine?*!

Esther was not worried about Mordecai being successful because she knew that his success in no way diminished the authority that was bestowed upon her as Queen, nor did it decrease her worth or value to the King. She still had power. She still had favor. And she did not lose sight of the fact that she still had a call on her life even though someone else was being blessed right in front of her. Just because the Father is blessing someone else does not mean that He has abandoned you! You will *never* stop being the apple of His eye, and there is nothing that anyone else in this world can do about that.

Not only does jealously speak volumes about how we see ourselves, but it also hinders us from joining together in unity! Later on in the chapter, the Bible tells us that both Esther and Mordecai come together and make a decree that would pinpoint the day that the Jews were delivered from mass genocide as a time of celebration known as the Festival of Purim. Now, what if Esther had become so jealous and intimidated by the success of Mordecai that she decided not to associate with him or help establish the Festival of Purim? How many opportunities for collaboration have you missed out on because you were jealous of your Sister?

Did you know that you are more dangerous to the enemy's territory when you join forces with your Sister than when you are separated from her? The enemy does not want unity amongst the people of God, especially the women, because he understands that the favor that we carry is detrimental to his kingdom. We are already powerful when we are by ourselves; but together, we are unstoppable.

Understand that, as Queen, there is a lane that is specifically crafted for you. And know that your Sister's elevation does not take away from the Father's love for you. You are of great value to Him, and there is nothing that can take that away from you.

Prayer

Father, I rebuke and renounce the spirit of comparison that has tried to negatively impact my life. Forgive me for looking at my sister with envy and jealousy. And forgive me for thinking that, because you were blessing other people, you had forgotten about me. Help me to realize that no one can beat me at being me and that when my sister succeeds, it is not a threat, but it is a time to celebrate. Help me to be able to show genuine and Godly love and support to my Sisters in Christ! Father, put me in contact with Godly women who will be able to encourage, uplift, and collaborate with me to do kingdom work. I am ready to join in unity with my Sisters for Your glory. I declare that the spirit of contentment with who You created me to be will rest on me from this day forward. And I thank you for helping me to never wish to be anything other than who You created me to be.

In Jesus's name, Amen.

Just in Case You Forgot

♥ You are called to love your Sister! (Matthew 22:39)
♥ If you truly love your sister, you will not envy her.
  (1 Corinthians 13:4)
♥ You cannot love God and have hate in your heart for
  your sister! (1 John 4:20)
♥ You should strive to join forces with your sister, not
  compete with her! (Ecclesiastes 4:9-12)

Notes

What Will You Leave Behind?

Esther 10:3 NLT. Mordecai the Jew became the prime minister, with authority next to that of King Xerxes himself. He was very great among the Jews, who held him in high esteem, because he continued to work for the good of his people and to speak up for the welfare of all their descendants.

Chapter 10 Breakdown

This is the final chapter of our beloved story. Sadly, there is nothing in this chapter written about Queen Esther.

A good Queen is known for *who she was*, but a great Queen is remembered for *who she served*. A true Queen is not measured by who she married, how beautiful she was, or how many children she had. No, a true Queen, is a servant first. And Esther had the heart of a servant.

I must admit that the last Chapter of the book of Esther definitely saddened me. This entire chapter was all about how great Mordecai became in the kingdom. And sure, that's nice and all; but I wanted to know what happened to our Queen?! What was the rest of her life like? What was her and the King's relationship like after everything settled down? Did Esther have any children? Details, Jesus, I need details?!

But then I realized, this is exactly how it should be. Yes, we are royalty and this entire book is geared towards how we can recognize our own value and significance, but at the end of the day, we must never lose sight of the fact that our primary focus is to serve the King of Kings and to help His people; not to make a name for ourselves. Just like Esther, when it is all said and done, we should not want the last chapter in our story to be all about us. No, the last chapter in our book should point directly back to the Savior.

Do not allow yourself to forget the true purpose for all of this. Our end goal is Heaven and our greatest assignment will always be to serve God. Through all of our ambitions and dreams, our primary desire should be to hear the Father say, "Well done, thou good and faithful servant!"

So, what do you hope to leave behind? When your time on this Earth is done, what do you want to be said about you? Do you want to be remembered for who you were, or do you want people to remember Who you served?

As you continue to embark on this journey towards recognizing the Queen inside of you, I pray that you will live a bold, confident, and limitless life before God. I pray that a fulfilled life, full of the joy, peace, grace, mercy and the strength of God is your portion. But most of all, my prayer for you, my Sister, is that when it is all said and done, you will let God have the last chapter in your story!

Now, my Sister, Dust that Crown Off.... Pick those Royal Garments Up... Keep God First... and walk into your destiny like the QUEEN that you are!

Prayer

Father, I ask that, in everything You would have me to do, please help it to make a positive impact on somebody's life! Let me be a world changer. If I am to be remembered, Father let it not be for the superficial things that I possess, but let it be for the way that I served You and Your people. Whatever You put in my hands to do, I will do it. Wherever You send me, I will go. Give me the desire to serve You Lord with all that is within me; not for my own glory, but for Yours. I pray that I will be able to apply all that I have learned while reading this book into my daily life. Help me to walk without fear and without doubt. Help me to be confident in Your love towards me. And let me never doubt that You are with me. I love You and I thank You for choosing me to go on this journey. Thank You for being with me every step of the way and I thank You for not only calling me Your daughter, but also for ordaining me as a Queen in Your Kingdom! May I bring Your name glory, honor and praise in all that I do and say.

In Jesus's name, Amen.

Just in Case You Forgot

♥ You were called for such a time is this! (Esther 4:14)
♥Your primary goal is to see Jesus and to dwell with him
  in eternity. (Psalm 27:4)

Notes

Afterword

Within the pages preceding this current thought, were given you clear, concise instructions to accept your Queenship in the Kingdom of God. The Lord placed within Queen Ariona, a burden for us women, to help us better understand our worth and call to royalty in Him. With great urgency, she chose to heed that call and obey the voice of the Lord. You are a direct beneficiary of her obedience and you now hold the knowledge that it will take for you to successfully go through your "process" of becoming Queen. Now that you have read each charge, taken notes, and affirmed yourself through prayer and scriptural reference, your "such a time as this" is at hand. But, just as any other call, the choice is yours to answer. God will not force you to accept the crown that has been set aside for you. No, He has given you control over the release of your "Yes."

You have been informed that you are to be Queen and reminded that you have no reason to fear. The seeds of power and authority have been planted within you and you have been equipped to defeat your enemy. But remember that none of those things are made relevant until you are first "purified". To be purified is to be cleansed. God has placed you in position to be cleansed of your past and anything that is trying to hinder you from taking your place in the kingdom. It is time to renounce each and every thing that would cause you to deny your royal lineage. "Haman" can't stop you, sis! Don't let him trick you into thinking that he can. No, your call spans far beyond what your mind can comprehend and what your eyes can see. Accept it!

I have learned, throughout the course of my life, more so recently, that I need my sisters to encourage, support, and sometimes, affirm me. What am I saying? As you've read, you need your sister's help, and she needs yours! There is a saying that goes, "Real Queens fix each other's crowns." Fix your sister's crown and walk alongside her. She is not your competitor. In fact, some say that "your biggest competition is who you were yesterday." Well, God's word says, in Philippians 3:13, to forget the things behind you and move forward. This means that you are not even in competition with yourself. Leave former you where she is. Queen Ariona told us that "Esther cannot wear Hadassah's rags and still be Queen!" You are Esther! You cannot wear the rags of your past and still be privileged to the crown of your future. So, walk in victory, for you have overcome your past. Walk in authority, for what you speak, you shall see. Walk in your purpose, on purpose, for you have been called.

You have been called out of darkness and into the light... the marvelous light, that is, as it states in 1 Peter 2:9. You were "fearfully and wonderfully made", as the Bible reminds us in Psalms 139:14. Let your story be written and give room for it to end with God, not your own works. As my sister, Ariona, reminded us, our last chapter should not be about us.

It's your time... you've been given a great charge. Wear the robe and accept the crown. Now, go forth, and become Queen.

- Alecia M. White -

black butterfly